PASSPORT TO

GERMANY

Keith Lye

Franklin Watts

London/New York/Sydney/Toronto

Original Edition 1986
Paperback Edition 1994

Published in Great Britain by
Franklin Watts
96 Leonard Street
London EC2A 4RH

Published in Australia by
Franklin Watts Australia
14 Mars Road
Lane Cove
NSW 2006

UK ISBN: 0 7496 0611 8 (hardback)
0 7496 1795 0 (paperback)

Editor: Chester Fisher
Design: Tony Truscott
Edward Kinsey
Illustrations: Hayward Art Group

Photographs: Chris Fairclough, ZEFA, Leslie Bishop, Braun, Camera Press, C.O.I. Photos, Zoë Dominic, German Federal Railways, German National Tourist Office, Robert Harding, Hutchison Library, Foto Jachsse, Keystone Press Agency, Lufthansa-Bildarchiv, The Mansell Collection, National Gallery, Popperfoto, Rex Features, Frank Spooner Pictures, C. Stadtler, ZDF

Front cover: ZEFA, Allsport

Printed in Belgium

Contents

DENMARK
Baltic Sea
Flensburg
Frisian Islands
Kiel
Rügen
North Sea
Rostock
Lübeck
Müritz Lake
Hamburg
R. Oder
Lüneburg Heath
Bremen
North German Plain
R. Weser
POLAND
Berlin
R. Elbe
Hanover
Brunswick
Magdeburg
THE NETHERLANDS
Münster
Bielefeld
Duisburg
Dortmund
Harz Mountains
R. Saale
Essen
Halle
R. Ruhr
R. Neisse
Düsseldorf
Leipzig
Dresden
Erfurt
Cologne
Aachen
Chemnitz
Bonn
BELGIUM
Ore Mountains
R. Rhine
Taunus Mountains
Wiesbaden
Frankfurt
LUXEMBOURG
R. Moselle
R. Main
Mannheim
Nuremburg
CZECHOSLOVAKIA
R. Neckar
Bohemian Forest
R. Danube
Karlsruhe
FRANCE
Stuttgart
Black Forest
R. Isar
0 20 40 60 80 miles
Augsburg
0 40 80 120 kms
R. Inn
Scale:1:2,500,000
Munich
Freiburg
AUSTRIA
SWITZERLAND
Alps

Introduction

Germany lies at the heart of Europe. It shares borders with nine other countries and has close ties with many of its neighbours. It has language links with Austria and Switzerland, and it works closely with Denmark, the Netherlands, Belgium, Luxembourg and France through the European Community.

For much of its history, Germany consisted of numerous small states. It became one country in 1871, only to be divided again after World War I. After World War II, Germany was divided into four zones. In 1949, the British, French and United States zones became West Germany, while the Soviet zone became a Communist country, East Germany. East and West Germany were reunited on October 3, 1990.

Germany has made a great contribution to European culture and has produced many great philosophers, musicians and writers. But the country suffered greatly in the 20th century through defeat in two World Wars, the oppression of the Nazi dictatorship, and post-war partition. After the country had been reunited in 1990, the German people faced the future with renewed confidence.

Above: Old traditions, such as the use of a towncrier of Lübeck, are preserved throughout Germany.

Below: The Berlin Wall, symbol of the divided Germany, was opened amid great excitement in 1989.

The land

Germany is a scenic country with varied landscapes, from snow-capped mountains in the south to a low coastal plain in the north. The main regions are the Bavarian Alps in the far south, the South German Hill Region, the Central Uplands and the North German Plain.

The Bavarian Alps run along part of Germany's southern border with Switzerland. They include the Zugspitze, the country's highest mountain, which rises 2,963 m (9,721 ft) above sea level. North of the mountains are the Alpine foothills, a beautiful region with many rivers, lakes and moors. The Bavarian Alps and the Alpine foothills attract many tourists.

The South German Hill Region contains long ranges of hills separated by fertile lowlands. The main rivers are the Rhine in the west and the Danube whose headwaters drain the southeast. The highest part of the region is the Black Forest, another tourist region with many health resorts, in the southwest.

Agriculture 52% **Urban and other uses** 19% **Forestry** 29%

Above: Although only 5 per cent of people work on the land, arable land and pasture cover more than half of Germany. Large areas of forest still exist.

Below: The ornate castle of Hohenschwangau overlooks the Alpsee and Schwansee, two of the many lakes in the Alpine Foothills.

The Central Uplands extend from Luxembourg in the west to the Ore Mountains and Bohemian Forest along the Czechoslovak border in the east. The highest parts of the Central Uplands are the Harz Mountains, which reach 1,142 m (3,747 ft), and the Thuringian Forest.

The North German Plain extends from the Netherlands border in the west to the Polish border in the east. It faces the North Sea in the northwest and the Baltic Sea in the northeast. This region contains many lakes and low hills made of moraine – rocks dumped there by the great glaciers (bodies of ice) that covered northern Germany in the Ice Age.

Germany has many rivers. The Rhine is the main north-south axis, flowing from Switzerland in the south, through south-western Germany, to the North Sea in the Netherlands. The Rhine flows through some magnificent gorges, with castles overlooking the river.

The most important river in the north is the Elbe, on whose banks stands Hamburg, one of Europe's largest seaports. Other major rivers include the Ems, Oder and Weser.

Above: The steep-sided valley of the Rhine near Bacharach in central Germany.

Below: This farm is in the Ore Mountains, south of Dresden.

The people

If you ask people from Munich to describe themselves, the chances are that they will say they are Bavarians rather than Germans. Until 1871 the area which now makes up Germany was a collection of separate independent states, and even today many of these regions still keep a sense of separate identity.

An example of these regional differences is that everyday speech heard on the street varies considerably from one area to another. Bavarians visiting the city of Cologne, for example, may have difficulty making themselves understood, and will themselves have difficulty with the dialect of Cologne. They will probably resort to using High German (*Hochdeutsch*). This is the standard language, as used in the media and in schools.

Most Germans are descended from the ancient tribes of the region, such as the Saxons and Frisians of the north, and the Bavarians and Swabians of the south. Although there has been much mixing of the groups over the centuries some original characteristics may have survived.

Above: Older Germans, like this couple, are likely to have experienced many dramatic changes in Germany during their lifetime.

Below: A shopping area in Dresden. Germans born since World War II are more informal in their dress and outlook than earlier generations.

Above: Hans Zimmermann sells sausages.

Below: Wolf-Dieter Löbe is a police officer.

Above: Waltraud Ettinger works in a florist's shop.

Below: Hermann Schäfer delivers the mail.

Northerners, it is said, are blue-eyed, sober and hardworking. Their towns are full of stern, brick buildings. By contrast, the southerners are of a darker complexion, and are thought to be more easy-going. Their buildings are often ornate and colourful. Regional differences are also reflected in religion: the north is mainly Protestant, the south Roman Catholic.

After World War II, many people moved from East Germany to West Germany, attracted by the higher standards of living and political freedom in the West. But from 1961 emigration from the East was severely restricted. From the 1950s, large numbers of foreign workers, called *Gastarbeiter* ('guest workers'), entered Germany mostly from Turkey, Yugoslavia and Italy.

In the early 1990s, the collapse of Communist rule in the countries of eastern Europe led thousands of other immigrants to enter Germany. They included people of German origin from Poland, Romania and Russia, together with refugees from other parts of eastern Europe.

Above: Gisela Thode manages a wine bar.

Below: Günter Hanisch, a foreign-language teacher.

Where people live

Germany is one of the world's most crowded countries. On average, there are 222 people to every square kilometre (574 to every square mile) of land. The most densely populated part of the country is the highly industrialized Ruhr area, which contains such cities as Essen, Dortmund and Düsseldorf. Other crowded regions include the suburbs of such cities as Berlin, the national capital, Hamburg, Munich, Cologne, Frankfurt am Main, Stuttgart, Bremen, Leipzig and Dresden.

As in other parts of Europe, the number of people working on the land has been declining, because agriculture has become more efficient and because more and more people are moving from rural to urban areas in search of work. In the early 1990s, only about five per cent of German workers were employed on farms. A movement of people from eastern to western Germany also occurred after the country was reunified, especially because of the collapse of many businesses and high unemployment in eastern Germany in the early 1990s.

Above: Germany is highly urbanized, with around 80 towns with populations of more than one million.

Below: Ranschbach is an old settlement in one of the wine-growing regions. All the houses cluster around the village church.

Left: Under Communist rule, Chemnitz was called Karl-Marx-Stadt.
Below: Munich, Germany's third largest city.

Above: Many Germans live in rented apartments, such as these in Mannheim, but most would prefer their own house.

Since Germany was reunified, Berlin has been Germany's largest city by far, with more than twice as many people as Hamburg, the second largest city. Germany has many other large cities, each being important for different reasons. For example, Frankfurt is a commercial centre, with many banks. Munich is a publishing centre with an important film industry, while Leipzig is known for its trade fairs. Hamburg, with its huge port, is one of Germany's great trading cities.

Many buildings were destroyed during World War II. A massive building programme took place in the 1950s and 1960s. Millions of new dwellings were built, especially in the cities. Many of them were in high-rise apartment blocks. As elsewhere in Europe, many people moved away from the inner city areas in the 1960s and 1970s. But this move to the suburbs has recently slowed down. Many young people are returning to live in the inner cities.

Berlin

Berlin became the capital of a united Germany in 1871. At the end of World War II, in 1945, the Allies divided the ruined city into four sectors, each one to be administered by one of the victorious powers – Britain, France, the USA and the USSR. Four years later the arrangements were changed and the USSR became responsible for East Berlin, and the other three powers for West Berlin.

As political tensions grew between eastern and western Europe, West Berlin found itself in an extraordinary position: it was entirely surrounded by the unfriendly new state of East Germany of which the eastern sector of Berlin was now the capital. West Berlin belonged to West Germany, whose capital was at Bonn, hundreds of miles away to the west. For a time, the only way westerners could reach West Berlin was by air.

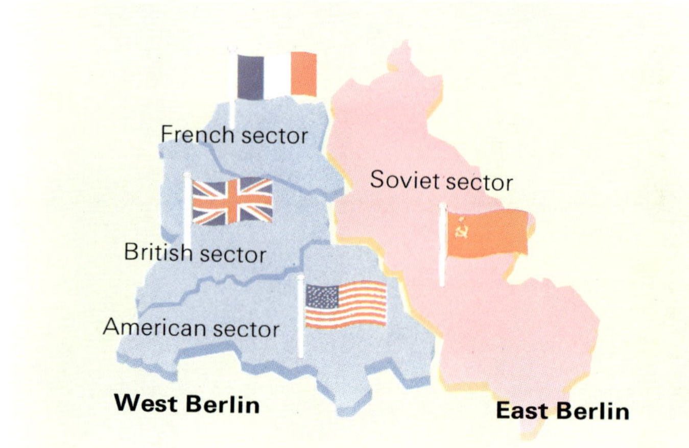

Above: Until 1989, Berlin was divided into four zones. After 1990, Berlin had a combined population of 3,377,000.

Below: The city of Berlin needed extensive rebuilding after World War II. Over half the city was destroyed but a few older buildings did survive.

Above left: Both Berliners and tourists like to shop in the Kurfürstendamm.

Above: Touring the city aboard the *Moby Dick.*

Below: The Pergamon Museum of ancient art is on Museum Island in what used to be East Berlin.

In August 1961 the East Germans built a wall right across the middle of Berlin, cutting themselves off from the West. The wall was heavily guarded and many East Germans died trying to cross it.

The decline of Communist rule in Eastern Europe led to demands for greater freedom. In 1989, all restrictions were lifted on travel and, finally, the hated, 28-year-old wall was opened. Berlin then became the national capital of the reunified Germany, though the parliament continued to meet in Bonn. United Berlin became one of the six states added to Germany by the reunification of the country.

Berlin is a lively city, famous for its opera, music, drama and cinema. It contains the University of Berlin, also called the Humboldt University, and the larger Free University. Landmarks include the Brandenburg Gate, topped by a statue of Nike, the Greek goddess of victory; the Kaiser Wilhelm Memorial Church, a memorial to World War II; a famous zoo; and the Soviet War Memorial. Berlin has broad shopping streets, lined with busy restaurants. The city also has many lakes and woodlands, where Berliners love to spend weekends.

Fact file: land and population

Key facts

Location: Germany, a nation at the crossroads between western and eastern Europe, lies between latitudes 47°30′ and 55° North and longitudes 6° and 15° East. It is bordered by nine other countries: Denmark, the Netherlands, Belgium, Luxembourg, France, Switzerland, Austria, Czechoslovakia and Poland. It has coastlines on the Baltic and North seas.
Main divisions: Germany consists of 16 states, including Berlin.
Area: 356,829 sq km (137,772 sq miles).
Population: 79,096,000 (1991 estimate). Germany has a larger population than any other European country, except for Russia.
Capital city: Berlin, though parliament meets in Bonn.
Major cities: (with English and German names and 1989 population estimates):
- Berlin (3,377,000)
- Hamburg (1,606,000)
- Munich (München, 1,218,000)
- Cologne (Köln, 940,000)
- Frankfurt am Main (629,000)
- Essen (621,000)
- Dortmund (589,000)
- Düsseldorf (570,000)
- Stuttgart (566,000)
- Leipzig (539,000)
- Duisburg (529,000)
- Dresden (516,000)
- Hanover (Hannover, 502,000)
- Nuremberg (Nürnberg, 482,000)

Language: High (Standard) German. German is one of the Germanic language family, which also includes Dutch and English.
Highest point: Zugspitze, 2,963 m (9,721 ft), on the Swiss border.
Major rivers: The Danube rises in the southwest and then flows east through seven countries before it reaches the Black Sea. The Rhine, Germany's most important river, rises in Switzerland. Its total length is 1,320 km (820 miles). The Oder and its tributary, the Neisse, form Germany's boundary with Poland.

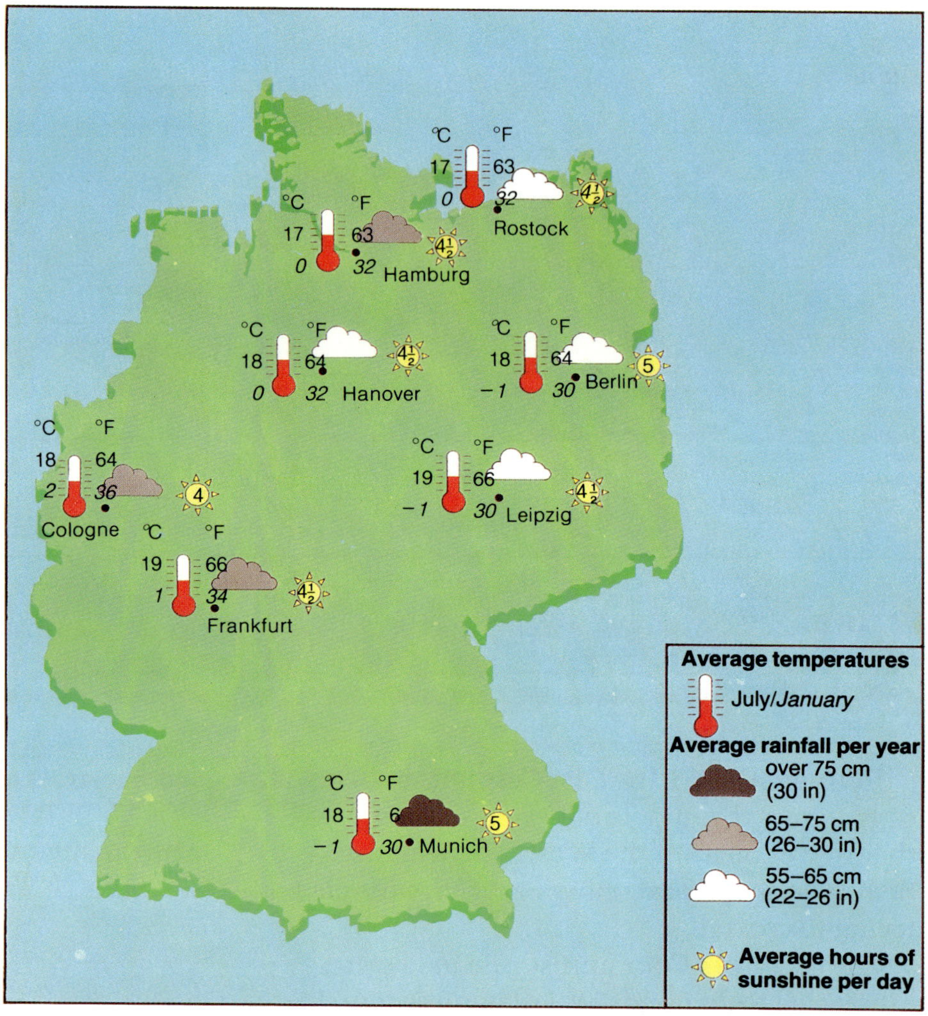

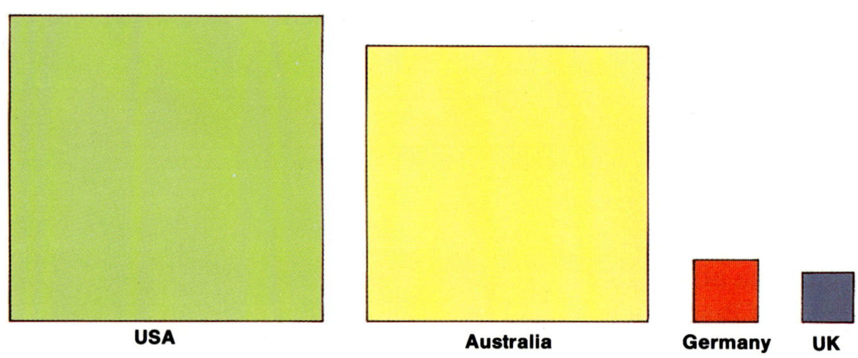

△ **A land area comparison**
Germany's land area of 356,829 sq km (137,772 sq miles) is small in comparison with many other countries. It is only about 1/26th of the size of the United States (9,370,000 sq km, 3,600,000 sq miles) and also much smaller than Australia (7,650,000 sq km, 2,470,000 sq miles). It is nearly $1\frac{1}{2}$ times larger than the United Kingdom (244, 030 sq km, 94,220 sq miles). The longest north-south distance in Germany is 853 km (530 miles). The longest east-west distance is about 560 km (348 miles).

▽ Germany's major cities, ports and routeways
Many of the large cities of Germany are located on the major rivers.

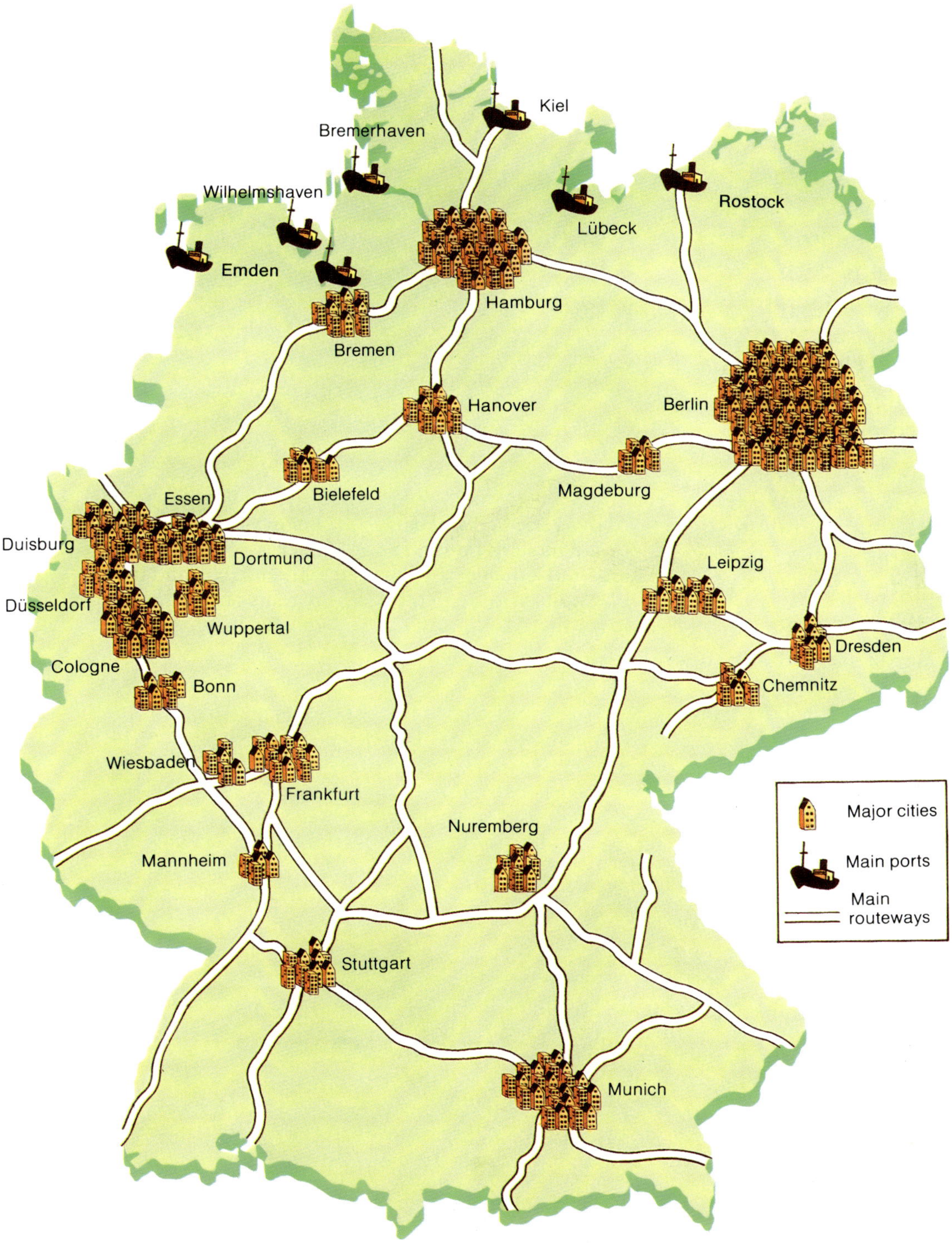

▷ A population density comparison
Germany has a high population density in both world and European terms.

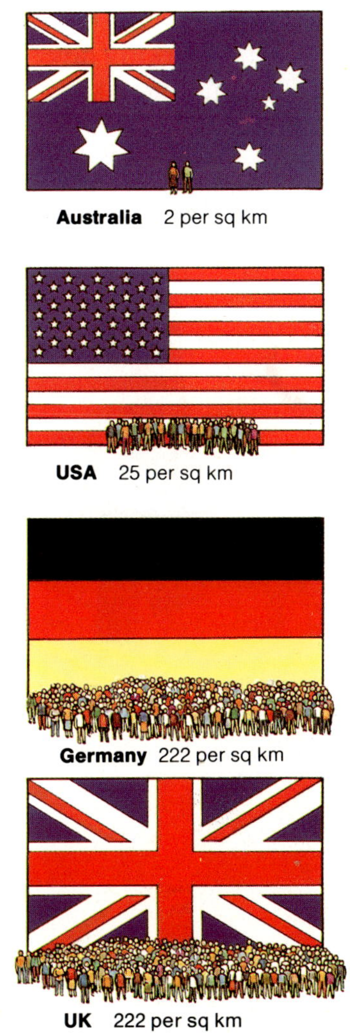

Home life

The Germans tend to be a home-loving people, and take great pride in keeping their houses neat and orderly. About 10 per cent of household income is generally spent on decorating and furnishing the home and both modern and traditional styles are popular.

Most families are small and live in compact houses and flats. Usually there is a kitchen, a bathroom, a living room and one or two bedrooms. Dwellings built in the last 15 years have been designed to a high standard, normally with central heating and with modern kitchens that include a refrigerator and a washing machine. Young children often share bedrooms. The traditional German bed-covering is a thick duvet or eiderdown known as a *Federbett*, which is soft, comfortable and very warm.

The working day starts early in Germany. Factories often start at about 7 a.m., and most shops, offices and schools are open by 8. So it is quite common for all the family to have left the house by half past seven in the morning.

Above: The Marschkes own a modern house on an estate outside Pliezhausen, a small town in southern Germany.

Below: The Marschkes's back garden, where the children play and their parents pursue their interest in gardening.

Left: As well as the living room shown here, the Marschkes's house has a dining room, four bedrooms, and a kitchen and bathroom.

Below: The two younger children, Simon and Silja, share a bedroom which also doubles as a playroom. Their elder sister Gundula has her own room, but still likes to use the playroom too.

Working hours tend to be quite long: an industrial worker, for instance, spends just over 40 hours a week at his or her job. There is, however, one consolation: Germany has many public holidays.

Most schools end between 12 noon and 1 p.m. and children go home to lunch. If the mother or father's place of work is close to home, they, too, will eat at home. After lunch the children will have homework to do, but once this is complete they can play or watch television.

Traditionally, the role of German women was confined to the three "K's": *Kirche* (church), *Küche* (kitchen) and *Kinder* (children). Today women are equal to men before the law, and account for approximately a third of the entire workforce. Even so, in many families it is still the male who is able to earn a higher salary and the woman who stays at home to do the housework and look after the children. As elsewhere in Europe, many German women are now challenging their traditional roles.

Shops and shopping

Germany was one of the very first countries to provide pedestrian precincts in town centres, areas where one can stroll from shop to shop without having to worry about traffic. Shopping centres often take in a mixture of large department stores and small specialized shops. Many Germans prefer the latter, because they offer goods of higher quality and more personal attention from the staff. Even the smallest gift will be elaborately wrapped.

From Monday to Friday, shops in Germany stay open until around 6 p.m. On Saturday most shops close at lunchtime, although on one Saturday each month they remain open until later.

Fruit and vegetables are usually bought from street markets which are held once or twice a week. Often it is the farmers themselves who set up the stalls, so everything is very fresh. Throughout December, many towns have special Christmas markets (*Weihnachtsmärkte*) with stalls selling everything from seasonal goodies to candles and Christmas trees.

Above: A selection of German packaged foods. Most families do the bulk of their shopping at the local supermarket.

Below: Nuremberg, like most other German cities, has a regular market where fruit and vegetables may be bought.

Above: A butcher's shop.

Left: There are about 1,500 types of German sausage.

Below: Clothes are often cheaper in department stores than in small shops, and there is usually more choice, too.

Supermarkets and hypermarkets are as popular as elsewhere in Europe and the USA, but small local shops continue to exist and have actually become more popular again in recent years.

The butcher's shop (*Metzgerei*) sells raw meat, as well as a variety of the sausages for which Germany is famous, and other cooked meats. The bakery (*Bäckerei*) normally bakes bread on the premises and offers a great range from crusty white rolls to rye bread and wholemeal loaves. For pastries, cakes and chocolates, one goes to a shop called a *Konditorei*. These shops often have a cafe attached to them, where one can sit down for coffee and cakes or a small snack. Most *Konditoreien* are open on Sundays.

Electrical goods are a particular bargain in many shops, with quality goods at low prices backed up with efficient servicing. Germany also has a long tradition of manufacturing and selling quality toys and the children's department of a big store often resembles an Aladdin's cave.

Cooking and eating

In Germany the day starts with a cup of fresh coffee and crisp rolls or sliced bread with butter or jam. Sometimes this light breakfast might include a boiled egg. Because people often have to leave home early in the morning, it is common to have a sandwich and a drink as a mid-morning snack.

The main meal of the day is usually eaten at lunchtime. Germans are fond of meat, particularly pork, and this is normally accompanied by potatoes or other vegetables such as puréed spinach, and salad. The evening meal is simple: a selection of cold sliced meats (*Aufschnitt*) is often served, together with different kinds of bread and cheese. This is washed down with beer or apple juice.

There are many special German dishes, some of which are associated with certain regions or particular times of the year. *Sauerkraut* is popular everywhere. It is a sort of pickled cabbage, and is often served with potatoes, sausages and dumplings which are known as *Knödl*.

Above: Ursula Marschke prepares a meal in her small but well-designed kitchen where everything is easily to hand.

Below: The Marschke family have a breakfast of rolls with jam or cheese. They have milk or coffee to drink.

Special dishes from the south include the famous *Weisswurst* sausages of Munich. Southerners are very fond of asparagus and of trout, and make elaborate cakes. The *Schwarzwälder Kirschtorte* (Black Forest Cherry Cake) has layers of chocolate sponge, spread with black cherry jam and whipped cream.

Along the northern coastline fish and seafood are popular, as is *Labskaus*, or salted meat. *Pumpernickel*, a very dark variety of rye bread, is often served with smoked ham. *Bohnensuppe mit Speck*, a thick bean soup with bacon in it, is just the thing for a winter's day. Lübeck, the port on the Trave River near its mouth on the Baltic Sea, is famous for its marzipan.

Take-away snacks are popular in Germany, especially sausages and french fries (chips) served with mayonnaise or ketchup. The Germans also enjoy eating out, and many towns have Italian, Greek and Turkish restaurants run by some of the immigrant families who have come to Germany.

Above: A street cafe situated in the city of Munich. Cafes usually serve light meals as well as drinks and snacks.

Below: Dieter Wetzel runs an hotel and restaurant near Stuttgart. As well as cooking, he must find time to welcome his guests.

Pastimes and sports

The mountains, forests and lakes of Germany provide a wealth of opportunity for outdoor activities. Even city dwellers normally have woodlands within easy reach, where they can go for a Sunday walk, or jog along the *Trimmdich-Pfade* or "keep-fit trails".

Towns of all sizes have open-air and indoor swimming pools: there are several thousand in Germany. In summer everyone who can flocks to the nearest river or lake or drives up to the north coast and islands for a day swimming or sunbathing on the beach. There are sailing boats, rowing boats and canoes everywhere and windsurfing is extremely popular.

The Germans are great gardening enthusiasts and will lovingly tend window-boxes and indoor plants even if they have no garden. Allotments (rented plots of land on which to grow vegetables) are to be found on the outskirts of most towns, and sometimes these include a small summer-house where one may spend evenings and weekends. Sundays are for visiting relatives or the countryside.

Above: Many Germans enjoy skiing on the fine ski slopes to be found in the mountains of Bavaria.

Left: At this popular North Sea resort, most of the families have hired "beach baskets". These provide shelter against the wind.

Left: The Germans are keen soccer fans, and millions of people watch the matches live or on the television. This game is taking place at Düsseldorf.

Soccer is Germany's most popular sport. Teams such as *Bayern Munich* are well known all over the world, and the German Football Association has more than four million members.

The second most popular sport, and the one with the longest tradition in Germany, is gymnastics. This is followed by shooting, athletics and handball. In 1985 the German tennis player Boris Becker won the Wimbledon men's singles championship at the age of only 17. Skiing is a popular winter sport in mountain regions. Such sports as horse-riding, which were once the privilege of the wealthy, now attract many Germans.

Every fourth German is a member of a sports club, or *Verein*. Even small villages may have a sports club whose members meet once a week and train in the gymnasium of the local school. Many youngsters join sports clubs as well, because many schools do not place great emphasis on sport.

Below: Germans enjoy both watching and participating in gymnastics. These girls are giving a display of synchronized trampolining at an open-air event.

News and entertainment

Publishing has long been an important industry in Germany. Printing was invented in Germany in the 15th century, and even today every tenth book published in the world is written in the German language. Books from all over the world are also translated into German: no wonder that reading rates as one of the Germans' most popular pastimes.

About 400 daily newspapers are published throughout Germany, including a number of tabloids, such as the *Bild Zeitung* of Hamburg. There are hardly any national daily newspapers. Most of Germany's famous quality newspapers, such as the *Kölner Stadt-Anzeiger*, are based on a large city.

Around 8,000 periodicals were published in the late 1980s, with circulations of more than 300 million. They range from political magazines, such as *Der Spiegel*, to motoring journals, women's and pop music magazines.

Above: Germany has a large number of bright and lively magazines which cater for young readers.

Above: Though there are many newspaper stalls in Germany, 75 per cent of all daily papers are ordered from newsagents.

Above: News and women's magazines are the most widely read of the 8,000 periodicals published in Germany.

Above: *Der Grosse Preis* is a television quiz programme which helps raise money for children's charities.

Left: Carolin Reiber the presenter of a popular music programme.

Right: A German television magazine.

Below: Young Germans like listening to many kinds of pop music. British and American groups have always been popular, but German pop stars also have many fans.

Germany is a land of television watchers. Around 90 per cent of all households own a television set and more than half of all Germans switch it on every day. There are three major channels, all managed by public corporations, which receive money from licence fees. There are also several regional television broadcasting corporations.

German television does feature commercials, but they only appear during the afternoon and early evening and they are never used to interrupt a programme. News, current affairs and excellent documentaries form a large part of television broadcasting time, but the most popular programmes tend to be films, entertainment shows and serials. Many of these are taken from British and American sources and the language is dubbed in German.

Many young people are interested in pop music and spend a lot of money buying the latest records. British and American groups have long dominated the pop scene, but in recent years many German groups have in turn made their mark on the German and international hit parades.

Fact file: home life and leisure

Key facts

Population composition: People under 15 years of age make up 16.0 per cent of the population; people between 15 and 59 make up 63.7 per cent, and people over 60 make up 20.3 per cent.
Average life expectancy at birth: 76 years (1990), as compared with 70 years in 1960. Women make up 51.9 per cent of Germany's population and, on average, women live six years longer than men.
Rate of population increase: In 1989–1990, the population of Germany was declining, with an annual growth rate of -0.2 per cent, despite immigration. The population has been stable or slightly declining since the 1970s.
Family life: The average household size in 1989 (for West Germany) was 2.2 persons. The average age at marriage was around 25 for men and 23 for women. Families are small. Most couples have one or two children.
Homes: About equal numbers of people live in houses and flats. Home ownership is low (especially in what was once East Germany).
Work: The average working week in what was West Germany was 40 hours in 1990. The average annual household income in 1989 was DM 50,984 (US $30,000). Incomes were lower in East Germany, but after reunification the government introduced economic policies aimed at raising incomes and living standards. The total workforce in Germany in 1990 was 38,883,000. The proportion of unemployed in former West Germany was about 5 per cent in 1991. In former East Germany it was 12 per cent--the result of rapid economic change.
Prices: The rate of inflation between 1965 and 1980 averaged about 5 per cent per year in West Germany. In the 1980s, the annual rate of inflation was 2.7 per cent per year, but in the early 1990s it rose again to more than 4 per cent in 1991.
Religions: About 43 per cent of Germans are Protestants and 35 per cent Roman Catholics. The Roman Catholics live mainly in the south.

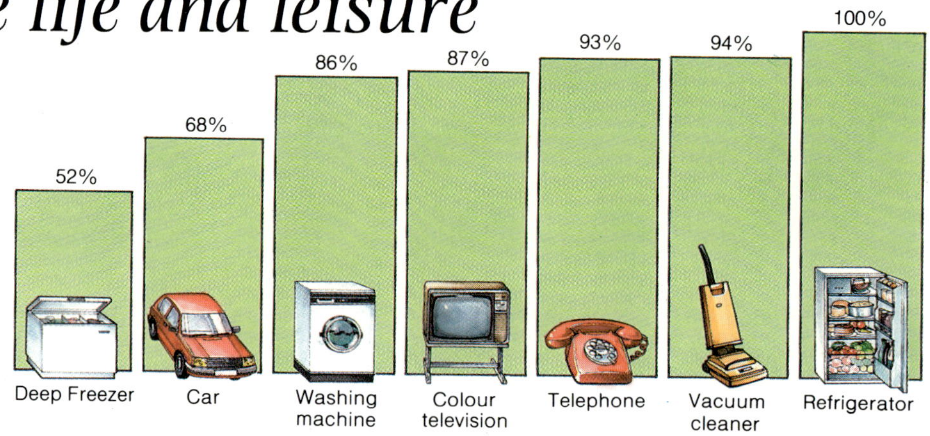

△ **The percentages of households owning various items in 1988**
Families in western Germany have acquired many household items which make life comfortable. No figures were available for eastern Germany in 1988.

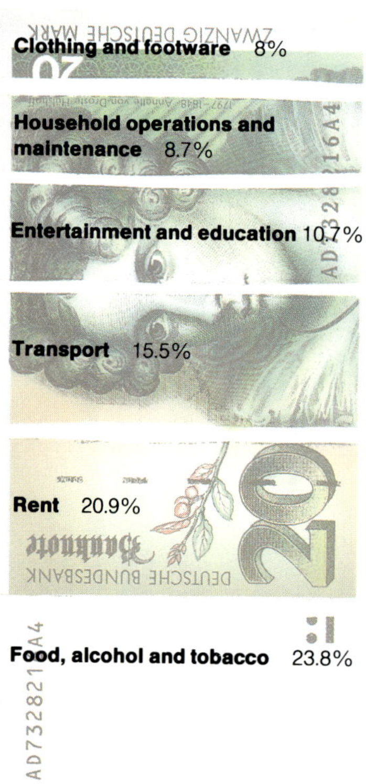

◁ **How the average household budget was spent in 1988**
In western Germany, people spend more income on food than most other Europeans. No figures were available for eastern Germany.

▽ **German currency and stamps**
The basic unit of currency is the Deutsche Mark (DM), which was introduced in 1948. It is divided into 100 Pfennigs. The Mark became the legal currency of East as well as West Germany on July 1, 1990.

△ **The most popular leisure pursuits in Germany**

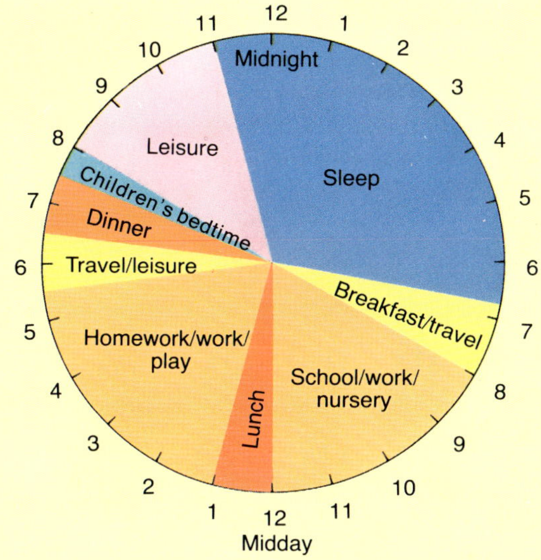

△ **How the average family spends a working day**

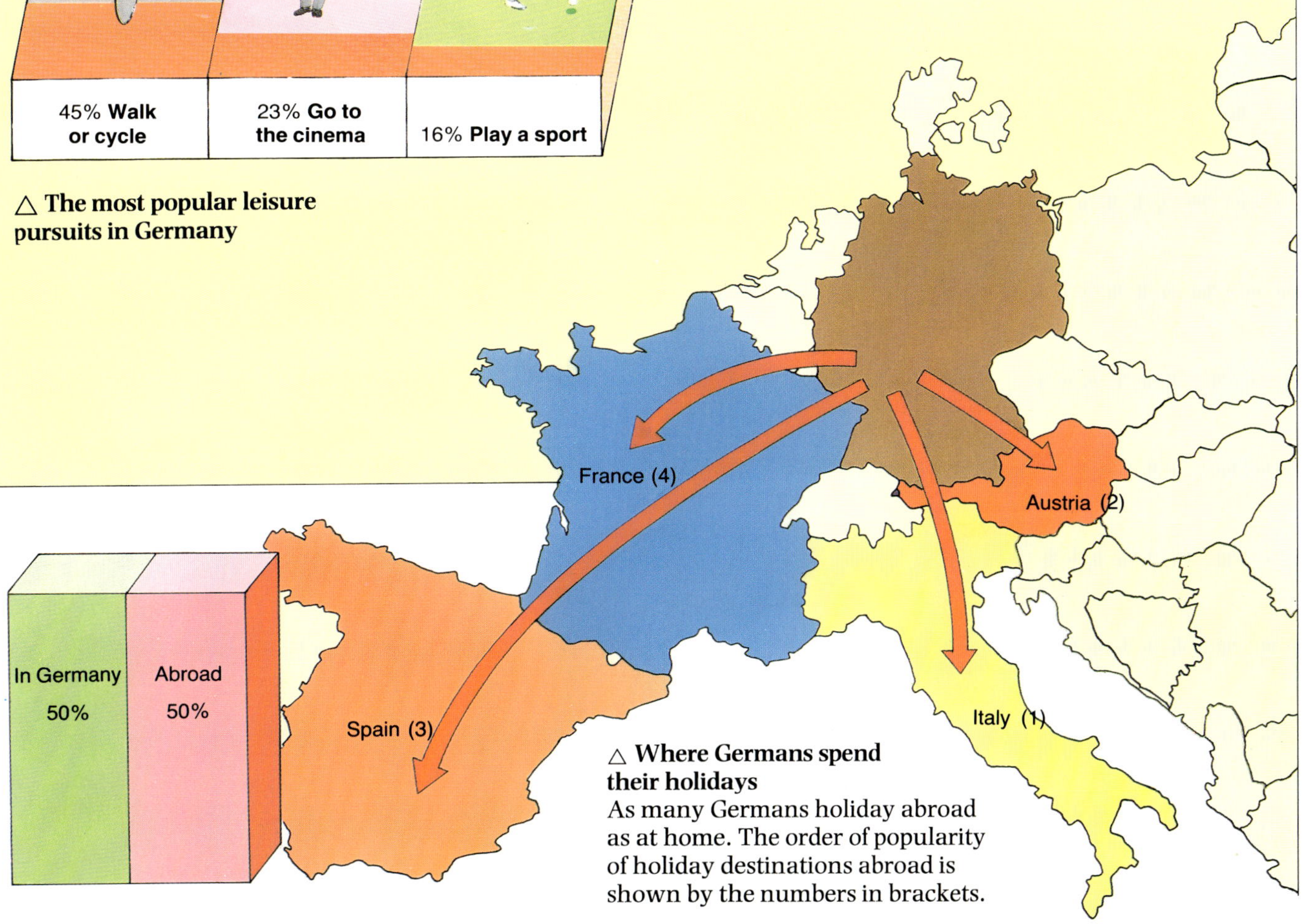

△ **Where Germans spend their holidays**
As many Germans holiday abroad as at home. The order of popularity of holiday destinations abroad is shown by the numbers in brackets.

Farming and forestry

The Germans make full use of almost all the land which can be farmed, but Germany has less fertile land than some other European countries and it has to import food.

The largest grassland areas are in the North German plain and in the foothills of the Alps. These areas are used mainly for grazing cattle. The northern region is best known for beef and milk production, the south for its cheeses, butter and other dairy products.

Central Germany is a mixture of forest, heath, arable land and grassland. It produces cereals and potatoes. The uplands are given over to mixed farming. The crops vary according to the soil and climate. They include wheat, rye, oats, potatoes and sugar beet. The land around Cologne and the foothills of the Harz Mountains are particularly fertile.

Along the Rhine, and the valleys of the Neckar, Nahe and Mosel (Moselle) rivers, the climate is generally mild, and the soil is suitable for fruit and vines. The vineyards rise in terraces along the sunny sides of the valleys.

Above: The Lanx family run a small farm in southern Germany. It is a mixed farm and they have both cereal crops and livestock.

Below left: Cheeses are an important product of the German dairy industry.

Below: Typical German livestock breeds.

Left: Before the country was reunified, East German farms were either large collectives, where people shared the produce, or they were state farms, where the government paid wages to the workers.

Below: These vineyards around the Kaiserstuhl, an old volcanic mountain in the Rhine valley, yield particularly good wine grapes.

Most farms in what was West Germany are small and some of them are operated part time. But most of them are highly mechanized and scientific. The farmers buy machinery through cooperatives they have set up with other farmers. In the early 1990s, the government began to divide up the large farms in the east which had been controlled by the government. Small plots were sold to individual farmers.

Although fewer people are working on farms, the efficiency of agriculture is increasing. Germany still has to import about a third of its food, but it is almost self-sufficient in wheat, oats, potatoes and dairy products.

In ancient times, dense forests of oak and other broadleaved trees covered Germany. Today the country is famous for its conifers. Forests cover about 20 per cent of the land and forestry is important. In recent years, pollution caused mainly by power stations burning coal and lignite has caused acid rain, which has killed many trees.

Resources and development

Germany has reserves of potash and salt, which are used in the chemical industry, and coal. The large coal reserves in the Ruhr region enabled Germany to become a great industrial power, but most of the high-quality deposits have been used up. Former East Germany has huge deposits of lignite, or brown coal.

The country has some oil and natural gas, but local supplies account for only a fraction of the country's needs. As a result, the country imports both oil, mainly from the Middle East, and natural gas. It also imports many of the metals needed by its manufacturing industries.

Coal-fired power stations in West Germany and lignite-fired power stations in East Germany (which have caused widespread pollution) once produced most of the electricity supply. But by 1990, nuclear power stations accounted for 34 per cent of the electricity produced in West Germany and 10 per cent in East Germany.

Germany also has many hydroelectric power stations, though the largest ones are in the south. Some are jointly operated with Austria and Switzerland.

Above: Lignite, or brown coal, is excavated at this open-cast mine in Garsdorf in the Ruhr district.

Below: This nuclear power station in north Bavaria helps to meet Germany's increasing energy demands.

Above: Well-known German car manufacturers' symbols.

Left: A view inside the BMW factory in Munich.

Below: East Germany's Trabant cars produced at Zwickau, near Chemnitz.

In 1945, Germany, defeated and divided, was in ruins and people were starving. However, with aid from the United States, West Germany recovered at such a fast rate that people described its revival as an "economic miracle". West Germany became the leading iron and steel producer in Europe. The steel was used for many products, especially cars and other transportation equipment. Other products include chemicals and textiles.

East Germany, which was an ally of the Soviet Union, had formerly been a mainly farming region. But it, too, developed quickly after World War II. It soon became one of the most industrialized countries in the Communist world, though its people were much less prosperous than those in West Germany. East Germany, whose manufacturing industries were run by the government, also produced iron and steel, machinery and transportation equipment. It had a major chemical industry.

Manufacturing

Most people from East and West Germany were delighted when their country was reunited in 1990. But the people of eastern Germany faced many problems. Many of their factories contained old machinery and they could not compete with generally cheaper and better-quality goods made in the modern factories in the west. Many factories in the east closed and unemployment increased quickly.

The German government set up an organization called *Treuhandanstalt*, which sought to reduce the role of the government in former East Germany, to increase the role of free enterprise, to make land available for new economic developments, and to encourage competition, so as to create new jobs.

Several West German companies, including the car-makers Volkswagen, BMW and Opel, electrical engineering companies Bosch, Siemens and AEG, and Pilz, a Bavarian firm producing compact discs, began to set up new industries in East Germany, while Zeiss of western Germany took over Carl Zeiss Jena in the east.

Above: This woman is packing hairdriers and their accessories on a Braun factory production line.

Below: This refinery which is situated near Mannheim is part of BASF, the largest chemical company in the country.

The restructuring of East Germany's economy created many problems and the cost for West Germans was greater than most people had expected. But Germany has a strong economy, and experts believe that it will become even stronger after eastern Germany's economy has been integrated with that of the west.

Germany's products are known throughout the world. Its best-known manufacturers are the car-makers, including Volkswagen, BMW, Daimler-Benz and Opel. Germany is the world's third largest car producer after Japan and the United States. The chemical industry, which produces such things as cosmetics, paints, plastics and medicines, is also important. Major companies include BASF, Hoechst and Bayer.

The electrical industry, including such well-known names as AEG, Bosch, Braun, Miele and Siemens, produces such things as television sets, hi-fis, computers and data-processing equipment. Textiles, precision instruments, china and glass are also major products.

Above: At the annual Hanover Trade Fair about 5,500 exhibitors display the newest industrial products.

Below: Burning lignite in power stations in eastern Germany, as here near Leipzig, has caused much pollution.

Transportation

Road transport is important and, in 1990, there was one car to every two people in western Germany and one car to every four people in the east. Germany was one of the first countries to build a motorway (*Autobahn*) network. It was begun in the 1930s and today only the United States has more motorways. Germany has more than 10,500 km (about 6,500 miles) of motorways, the densest network in the world.

In 1989, about 34 million cars and 1.7 million lorries and buses were on the roads. Most people in the west go to work in their car and, on public holidays and in the summer, the *Autobahnen* are congested, partly because of local traffic, and partly because they are used by motorists from other north European countries who want to travel south.

The Federal German Railway (*Deutsche Bundesbahn*) has 56,560 km (about 35,150 miles) of track, connecting all parts of the country. It provides excellent services for both freight and passengers, who numbered about 1,720 million in 1989.

Above: The bulk of Germany's freight is carried by road. Germany has one of the world's busiest networks of motorways, called *Autobahnen*.

Below: German railways are being modernized, and people are being encouraged to travel by train rather than use private cars.

Cross-country buses are usually run by the railway company or by the post office (*Deutsche Bundespost*). Within towns there are municipal bus services and trams (*Strassenbahnen*). An increasing number of cities have an underground (*U-Bahn*) network, which is often an extension of the existing tram system. There are no conductors on trams and buses and one has to buy tickets from a machine before starting a journey.

The national airline is Lufthansa, which was 51 per cent government-owned in 1990. Lufthansa is based in Frankfurt am Main, which has one of Europe's largest and busiest airports. Other major airports are in Berlin, Düsseldorf, Hamburg, Leipzig and Munich.

Germany has more than 7,500 km (4,660 miles) of inland waterways. Canals and rivers, especially the Rhine, are busy with tugs and strings of barges, as well as pleasure craft. Major seaports include Hamburg, Bremen and Wilhelmshaven.

Above: The airport at Frankfurt am Main was the third busiest international airport in 1990. About 29 million passengers passed through.

Below: The Rhine is one of Germany's leading waterways. Barges carrying materials and manufactures pass through some superb scenery.

Fact file: economy and trade

Key facts

Structure of production: Of the total West German GDP in 1990 (the value of all economic activity), farming, forestry and fishing contributed 2 per cent, industry 41 per cent, and services 57 per cent. (No comparable figures existed for the east.)
Farming: Farmland covers roughly half of Germany. *Main products:* Barley, wheat, fruit, wine grapes, hops, oats, potatoes, rye, sugar beet. *Livestock:* Cattle, 20,538,000; pigs, 25,012,000; sheep, 4,649,000; poultry, 121,465,000.
Forestry and fishing: Forests cover about a fifth of Germany. The fish catch in 1989 was 408,200 tonnes, including Atlantic herring (25 per cent), Atlantic cod (14 per cent) and trout and salmon (6 per cent).
Mining: Germany is the eighth largest coal producer and it ranks first in lignite (brown coal) production. Potash, salt, some iron ore and oil are also mined, but Germany imports oil and many metals.
Energy: Coal-fired power stations produced 50 per cent of the electricity in western Germany in 1990 and nuclear power stations 34 per cent. In eastern Germany, lignite-fired power stations supplied 73 per cent and nuclear power stations another 10 per cent.
Manufacturing: Germany is one of the world's leading industrial nations, together with the United States and Japan.
Transportation: *Roads:* 220,855 km (137,237 miles), including 10,576 km (6,572 miles) of *Autobahn*; *Rail:* 56,560 km (31,150 miles); *Shipping:* The merchant fleet included 1,551 ocean-going vessels in 1990. *Air:* The national airline is Lufthansa.
Trade (1990): *Total Imports:* US $337,341 million; *exports:* US $400,504 million. This makes Germany the world's second most important trading nation.
Economic growth: The average growth rate of West Germany's gross national product in 1960–1990 was 2.4 per cent per year. No comparable figures exist for East Germany.

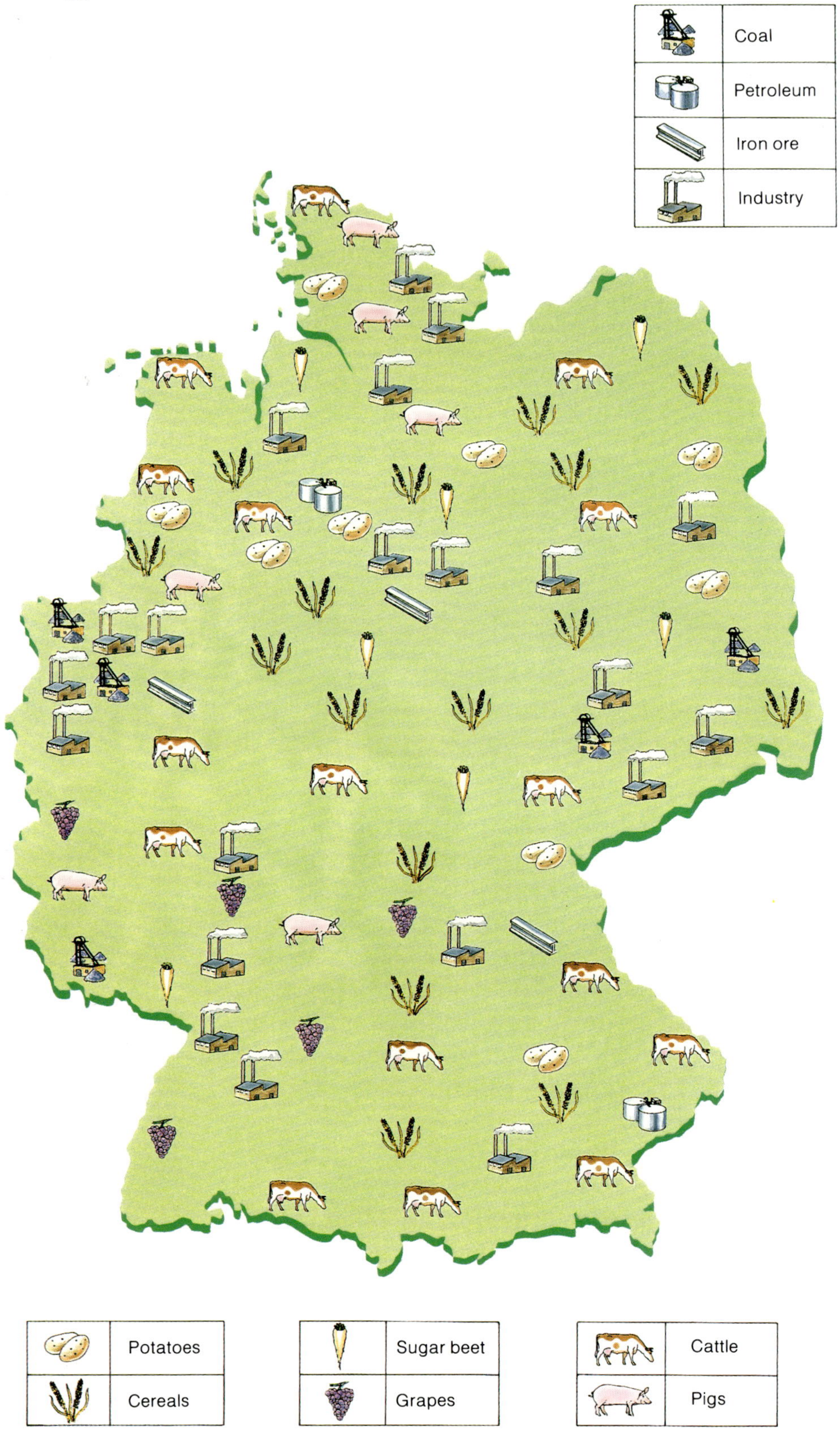

△ **The distribution of economic activity in Germany**

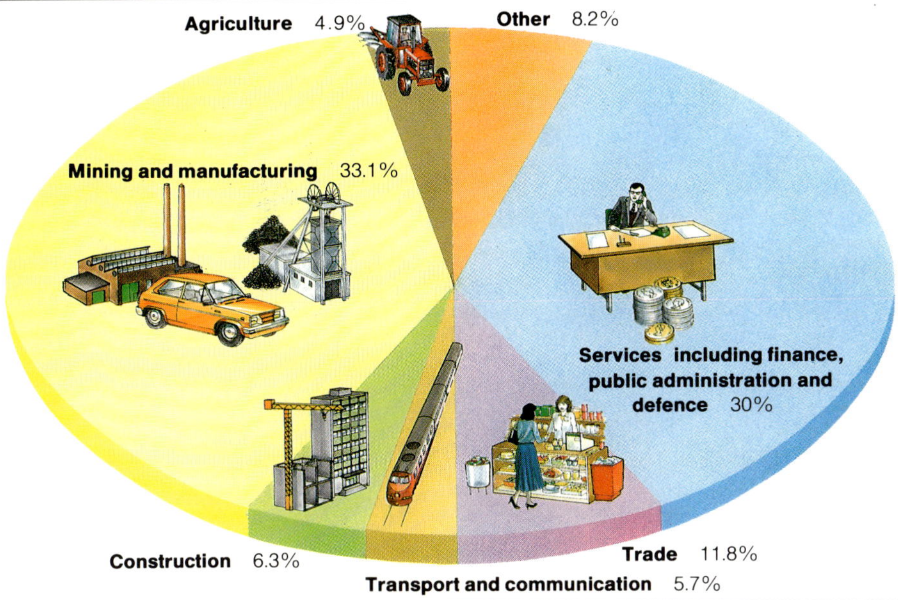

◁ **The percentages of the workforce employed in various industries in 1990**
When Germany was reunified, the pattern of employment differed considerably between East and West. For example, about three times as many people worked in farming in East Germany as compared with the West. Economic changes in the early 1990s soon began to narrow these gaps.

▷ **Germany's main trading partners in 1990**
The countries of the European Community are Germany's main trading partners, though before reunification most of East Germany's trade was with the former Soviet Union and Communist Eastern Europe.

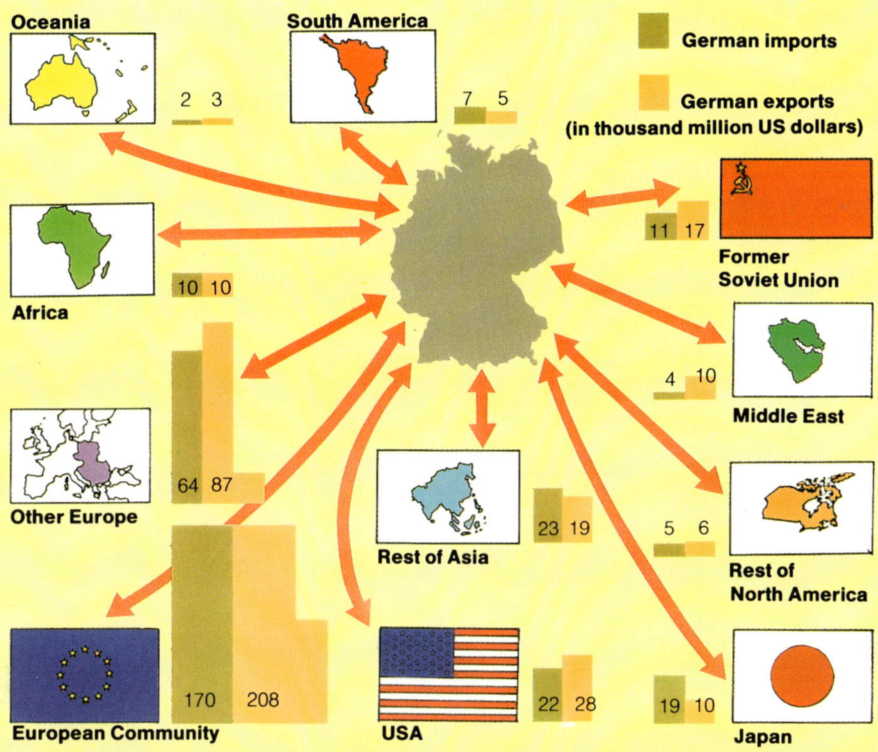

▽ **The types of items imported and exported by Germany in 1990**
Germany imports raw materials and food. These imports are balanced by large exports of manufactures, including vehicles and engineering products.

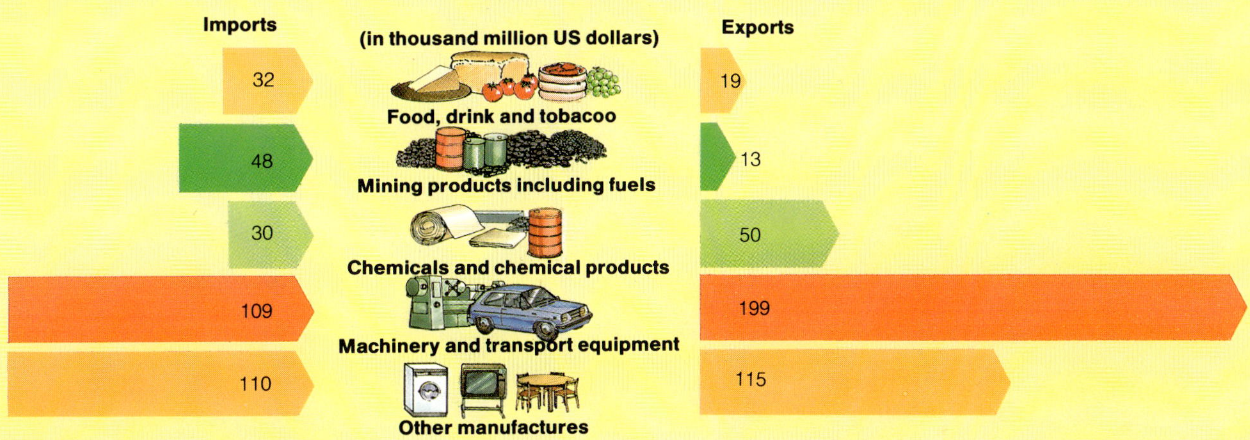

Education

Education in Germany is organized individually by each of the 16 Federal States. The type of school attended by a child, and what he or she learns there, depends on where the school is located.

Even so, the broad pattern remains the same throughout the country. Education is free for everyone from primary school through to university. All children have to attend school for 12 years, of which nine need to be full time, and of which the last three can be part time. Schools are often run on informal lines; there are no school uniforms and children are encouraged to be independent.

The first four years of school are spent at primary school (*Grundschule*). There are then several options. In order to postpone a decision, many pupils now spend their fifth and sixth years in a so-called "orientation grade". Some then opt for intermediate schooling in a *Realschule* which takes six years and leads to an exam for entrance into technical college.

Above: When the weather is fine pupils spend their breaks in the yard in front of their large modern school situated north of Munich.

Below: These children at a school in Cologne are taking part in an English lesson. All Germans must study a foreign language at school.

Left: These apprentices at vocational school are studying the properties of some of the materials used in the printing industry.

Below: Bonn University was founded in 1786. There are about a million students at German universities, which is more than five times the number in the early 1960s.

About half of all pupils go on to a short-course secondary school (*Hauptschule*) until they are 15 years old, when they take up a vocational apprenticeship (*Lehre*). These last three years and there are about 450 professions to choose from. Most of the training is on the job, but there are also lessons on general subjects, such as German, English and mathematics, as well as on the theoretical side of the work.

Would-be teachers or university students must go to a grammar school, or *Gymnasium*. Some of these specialize in the arts, others in sciences, but they all require nine years' attendance before taking the final *Abitur* exam. The top class, or *Oberprima*, will, therefore, often have pupils who are 20 years old or more.

Some Federal States have introduced comprehensive schools (*Gesamtschulen*) for all pupils from the fifth school year onwards. Free comprehensive school education for ten years is the system used in the states which formerly made up East Germany.

The arts

Probably no other country has produced as many outstanding composers as Germany. Johann Sebastian Bach (1685–1750), Ludwig van Beethoven (1770–1827) and Richard Wagner (1813–83) are just a few of the many famous names to be associated with classical music. Today, music remains a popular part of German cultural life. Even small towns have concert halls, and often a municipal orchestra as well. Major orchestras, such as the Berlin Philharmonic, are internationally famous.

Those who prefer dramatic arts also have no lack of choice. Almost all of the theatres in Germany are publicly owned and are subsidized so that they do not have to support themselves solely by the sale of tickets. Each year around 17 million people go to see a play in Germany. The classical German playwrights are Johann Wolfgang von Goethe, whose greatest dramatic achievement was *Faust*, Johann von Schiller (1759–1805) and Gotthold Ephraim Lessing (1729–81), and their works are the ones most frequently performed.

Above: Ludwig van Beethoven ranks as one of the greatest classical composers. He wrote symphonies, concertos and chamber music.

Left: A scene from the opera *Tannhäuser*. This was written by Richard Wagner, the master of German romantic opera.

German writers are probably less well known than German composers, though the literature is very rich, and every century has produced some outstanding works. Bertolt Brecht (1898–1956) and Thomas Mann (1875–1955) are the best known this century, and their books have been translated into many other languages. During the Hitler regime the arts were suppressed generally, so the end of World War II marked a new beginning, with writers such as Günter Grass (1927–) and Heinrich Böll (1917–85) becoming popular.

Although there is no great tradition of German painting, a few artists, such as the Renaissance painter Albrecht Dürer (1471–1528) produced outstanding works. There was also an important painting revival, the expressionist movement, at the beginning of the 20th century.

In recent years films from Germany have begun to reach international acclaim. *The Tin Drum* and *The Marriage of Maria Braun*, for instance, have been shown in many countries throughout the world.

Above left: The poet and playwright Goethe (1749–1832).

Above: Albrecht Dürer's painting *The Virgin and Child*.

Below: Despite war-time losses, some of Germany's fine architecture survived. The famous Gothic cathedral in Cologne was started in 1248, but was not completed until 1880.

The making of modern Germany

Until the middle of the 19th century, Germany consisted of numerous separate states. During the middle years of the century, the state of Prussia, under Wilhelm I and his prime minister Otto von Bismarck, became the leader in the move towards unification. After a series of wars in which Prussia and its allies annexed parts of Denmark, Austria and France, Germany was finally united in 1871. Wilhelm I became Emperor of the new German Empire. Under Wilhelm II (1888–1918), Germany was led into a disastrous war in 1914.

World War I (1914–18) ended in defeat for Germany and her allies. The Empire ended, and Germany became a republic. In 1919 a new constitution was drawn up but the republic never reached a firm footing. It collapsed in 1929, during the world economic crisis. No majority capable of governing could be found, and the previously almost unknown National Socialist movement under Adolf Hitler grew to be the strongest party within two years.

Above: Bismarck was known as the "Iron Chancellor". He held much power in Germany in the second half of the 19th century, but was not a democratic leader.

Left: The prospect of a unified Germany was a threat to France, and one of the reasons for the Franco-German war in 1870. Here the Prussian artillery are laying siege to the city of Strasbourg.

Left: A German soldier at an observation post in World War I. Nearly two million German soldiers were killed in this war.

Above: Adolf Hitler (1889–1945).

Below: World War II left Berlin in ruins.

In January 1933 Hitler became Reich Chancellor and he proceeded to give himself almost unlimited power. Opposition parties were banned and citizens' freedoms were strongly curtailed. Political opponents and Jews in particular were persecuted. Those who did not manage to escape were taken to concentration camps where millions of them were killed. In spite of all this there was very little opposition to Hitler's dictatorship because he had promised the Germans an improved economy and no more unemployment.

It was Hitler's aim to conquer all of Europe, and his attack on Poland in September 1939 marked the beginning of World War II. Although the German army was successful early in the war, it soon began to suffer serious losses. However, the war continued until April 1945 when the entire country was occupied by enemies. Hitler killed himself and Germany surrendered to the Allied Powers who divided it into four military occupation zones. It was an enormous defeat and left the country in ruins.

Germany in the modern world

In 1949, the American, British and French zones were combined as the Federal Republic of Germany (popularly called West Germany). The Soviet zone became the German Democratic Republic (East Germany). Ultimate power still remained in the hands of the occupying powers until 1955, when both West and East Germany became officially independent.

The West Germans quickly rebuilt their country and their economy boomed. East Germany also recovered quickly, though its growth lagged behind West Germany's. After nearly three million East Germans had emigrated to the west, East Germany strengthened its boundaries. In 1961, the East Germans built a wall through Berlin. Political tension between the two Germanies increased. But in the late 1980s, sweeping changes occurred throughout Communist eastern Europe

In 1989, many East Germans organized protests against their Communist government, while many others began to move to the west. Finally, the Berlin Wall was opened in October 1989 amid scenes of great jubilation.

Below left: In recent years Turks and other immigrant workers have protested about their poor living conditions.

Above: Adenauer (right) meets De Gaulle in 1963. **Below:** Chancellor Kohl and British Prime Minister John Major at an Economic Summit in 1992.

Left: Huge crowds celebrated in Berlin and other parts of Germany on the evening of October 2, 1990, before the reunification of East and West Germany on October 3.

Above: Pollution is a problem in many German rivers.

Below: This German street shows many foreign influences.

Free elections were held in East Germany in March 1990. Most of the candidates favoured the reunification of Germany. By mid-1990, the East Germans had begun to privatize (sell off to private owners) many government-owned businesses. In July, West Germany's Mark became the official currency in the east. Finally, East and West Germany signed a unification treaty and, on October 3, 1990, the German Democratic Republic ceased to exist.

The first national elections in the reunified Federal Republic of Germany were held in December, and Helmut Kohl, West Germany's Chancellor since 1982, continued as Chancellor of the reunited country. The delight of Germans at reunification was soon tempered when people in the west had to pay higher taxes to help finance the drastic changes in the economy in the east, and many easterners lost their jobs. But despite the problems, most Germans looked forward to a prosperous future.

Fact file: government and world role

Key facts

Official name: *Bundesrepublik Deutschland* (Federal Republic of Germany).
Flag: Three horizontal bars of black, red and gold.
National anthem: The third verse of *Deutschland-Lied*.
National government: *Head of State:* The President, who is elected by the Federal Convention for a term of 5 years. *Head of the government:* The Federal Chancellor, who is proposed by the President and elected by the *Bundestag*. *Parliament:* Parliament consists of two houses. The 662 members of the Federal Diet (*Bundestag*), the more powerful of the houses, are directly elected to terms of four years. The Federal Council (*Bundesrat*) consists of 68 members appointed by the governments of the 16 states, or *Länder*. Most legislation passed by the *Bundestag* must then go to be approved by the *Bundesrat* before it finally becomes law.
Local government: Each of the 16 *Länder* has its own regional government and legislature, most of whose members are elected to four-year terms. The number of *Länder* was increased on reunification when the former states of East Germany (Berlin, Brandenburg, Mecklenburg-Western Pomerania, Saxony, Saxony-Anhalt, and Thuringia) were included.
Armed Forces: *Army:* The strength of the Army in 1988 was 488,400. On reunification, 50,000 personnel from the former East German Army were integrated into the Germany Army. *Air force:* The Air Force consisted of 106,000 people in 1990. *Navy:* The Navy had 38,000 personnel in 1990.
Economic alliances: In 1957 West Germany was a founder member of the European Economic Community (now the European Community). The 12-member EC is now the world's largest trading block.
Political alliances: Germany is a member of the UN, the Council of Europe and, since 1953, the North Atlantic Treaty Organization (NATO).

◁ **The 16 German states, or Länder**
On reunification in 1990, the number of German states was increased to 16. This includes three cities – Berlin, Bremen and Hamburg – which are also states. The largest state is Bavaria, which covers 70,546 sq km (27,238 sq miles).

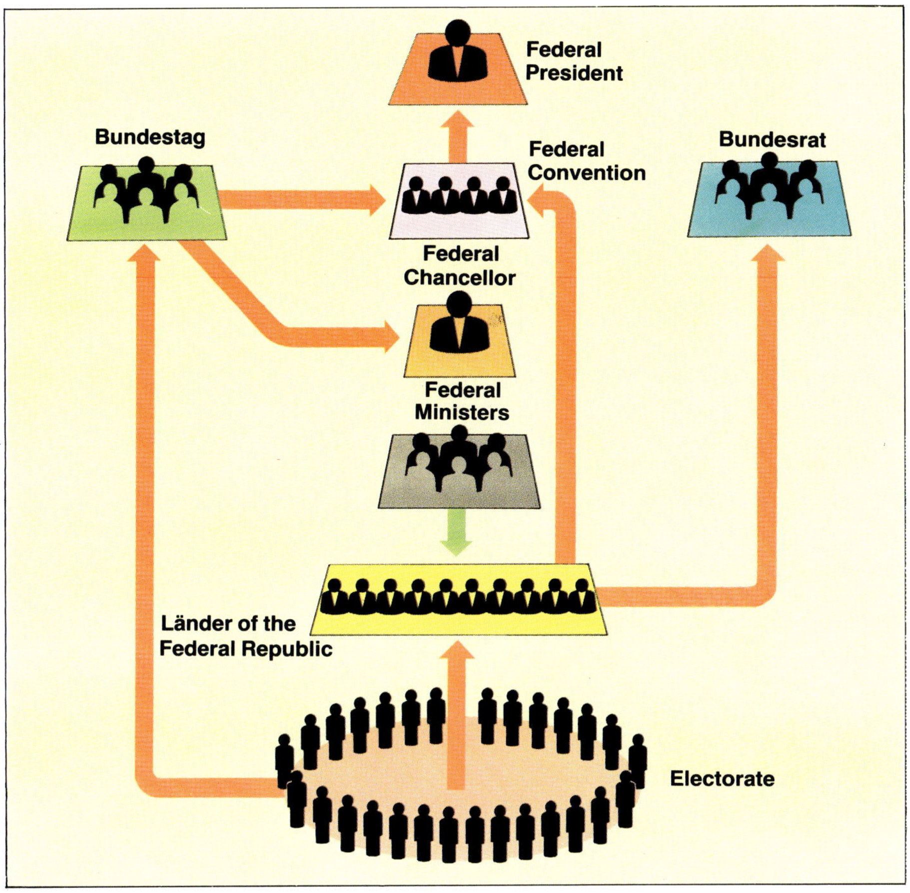

◁ **The government of Germany**
Germany's federal system of government is similar to that of the United States. The *Länder* (or States) have wide powers, but some major functions, such as defence, are controlled by the federal government. The Federal Chancellor is the leader of the largest party in the *Bundestag* (Parliament).

▽ **The European Economic Community**
The EEC has now grown from six to twelve members. Many trade barriers have been abolished between members, and there are common policies for agriculture and fisheries.

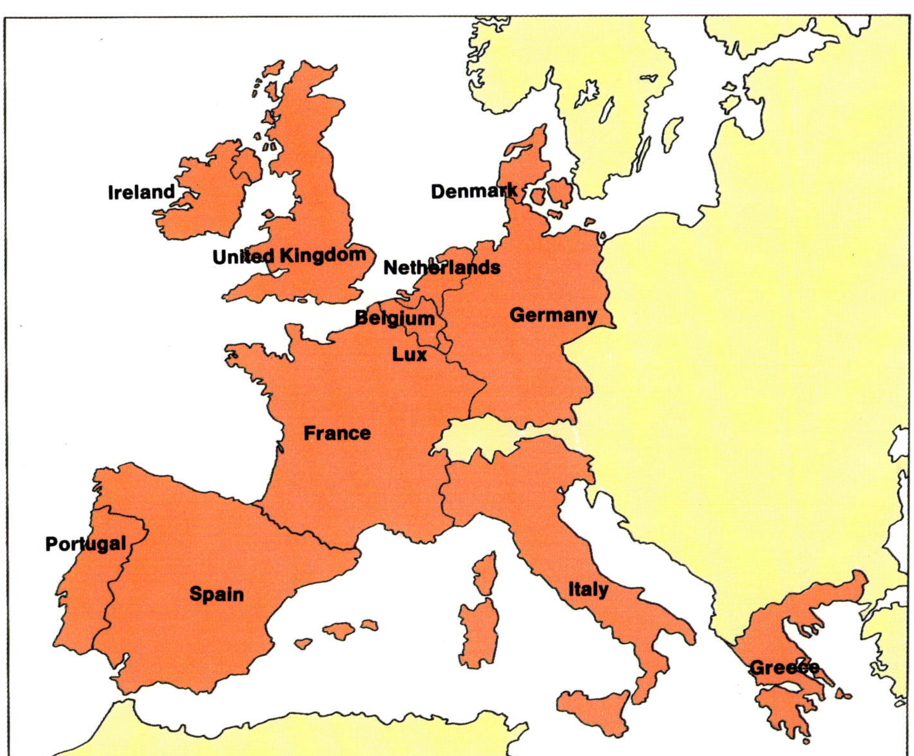

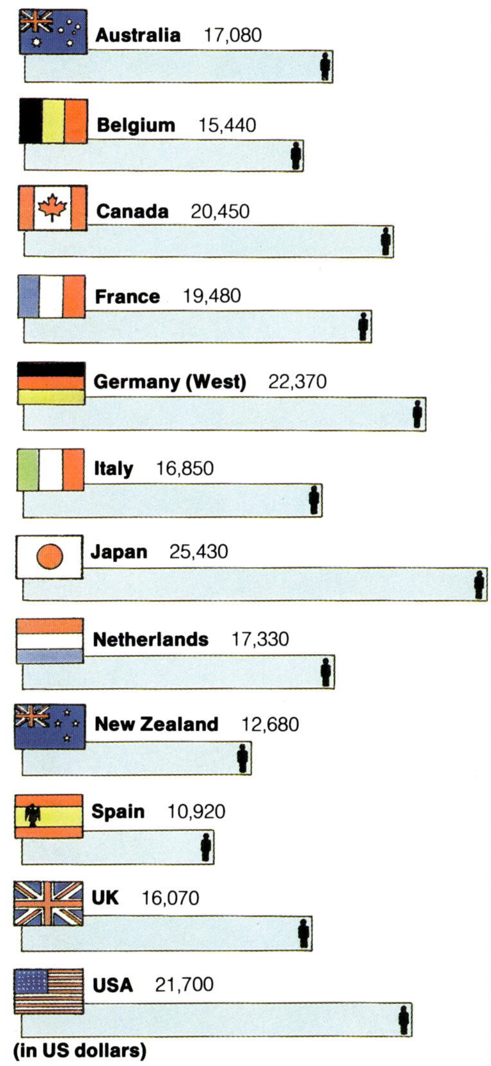

△ **National wealth created per person in 1990**
The figure for Germany is for West Germany only. This is because comparable figures were not available for the region that was East Germany, where the economy was in a state of rapid change.

Index